BIG SPORTS BRANDS
GATORADE
Sports Drink Innovator

By Rebecca Rowell

SportsZone

An Imprint of Abdo Publishing
abdobooks.com

abdobooks.com

Published by Abdo Publishing, a division of ABDO, PO Box 398166, Minneapolis, Minnesota 55439. Copyright © 2024 by Abdo Consulting Group, Inc. International copyrights reserved in all countries. No part of this book may be reproduced in any form without written permission from the publisher. SportsZone™ is a trademark and logo of Abdo Publishing.

Printed in the United States of America, North Mankato, Minnesota.
052023
092023

THIS BOOK CONTAINS RECYCLED MATERIALS

Cover Photo: Aaron M. Spreche/AP Images
Interior Photos: Kevin Sabitus/Getty Images Sport/Getty Images, 4–5; Mike McGinnis/Getty Images Sport/Getty Images, 7; Billie Weiss/Boston Red Sox/Getty Images Sport/Getty Images, 8; Sam Greenwood/Getty Images Sport/Getty Images, 10–11; HC/AP Images, 13; John Jones/Icon Sportswire/Getty Images, 14; Lynn Pelham/Sports Illustrated via Getty Images/Sports Illustrated Classic/Getty Images, 15; Peter Read Miller/AP Images, 16; Patti McConville/Alamy, 19; Shutterstock Images, 20–21, 25; Billy F Blume Jr/Shutterstock Images, 23; Igor Golovniov/Shutterstock Images, 27; Mark Elias/AP Images, 28–29; RacingOne/ISC Images & Archives/Getty Images, 31; Gary Newkirk/Allsport/Hulton Archive/Getty Images, 33; Douglas P. DeFelice/Getty Images Sport/Getty Images, 34–35; Zach Bolinger/Icon Sportswire/Getty Images, 37; Brian Garfinkel/AP Images, 39; Denis M Art/Shutterstock Images, 41 (left); Yeti Studio/Shutterstock Images, 41 (right)

Editors: Steph Giedd and Priscilla An
Series Designer: Joshua Olson

Library of Congress Control Number: 2022949053

Publisher's Cataloging-in-Publication Data

Names: Rowell, Rebecca, author.
Title: Gatorade: sports drink innovator / by Rebecca Rowell
Other title: sports drink innovator
Description: Minneapolis, Minnesota: Abdo Publishing Company, 2024 | Series: Big sports brands | Includes online resources and index.
Identifiers: ISBN 9781098290689 (lib. bdg.) | ISBN 9781098276867 (ebook)
Subjects: LCSH: Gatorade (Firm)--Juvenile literature. | Sports--Equipment and supplies --Juvenile literature. | Brand name products--Juvenile literature. | Beverage industry--Juvenile literature.
Classification: DDC 658.827--dc23

TABLE OF CONTENTS

Chapter One
THE WORLD'S SPORTS DRINK 4

Chapter Two
FOUNDED IN RESEARCH 10

Chapter Three
ENERGY DRINKS AND MORE 20

Chapter Four
FOCUSED ON ATHLETES 28

Chapter Five
CONNECTING WITH CONSUMERS 34

TIMELINE 42
IMPORTANT PEOPLE 44
GLOSSARY 46
MORE INFORMATION 47
ONLINE RESOURCES 47
INDEX 48
ABOUT THE AUTHOR 48

Chapter One

THE WORLD'S SPORTS DRINK

It was another hot August day. School had not started yet, but the high school football team had been getting together for at least two hours every day. After a few months of enjoying summer vacation, the players were getting back into shape. They were running laps around the field to build up their endurance.

The young athletes were eager to be done. They were tired, sweaty, and thirsty. Heading down the final stretch, Charlie kicked into high gear. He decided to sprint to the end. Derrick, his best friend, was at his side. The teens huffed and puffed, pushing forward.

Gatorade is found on the benches at many sporting events, including football and basketball games.

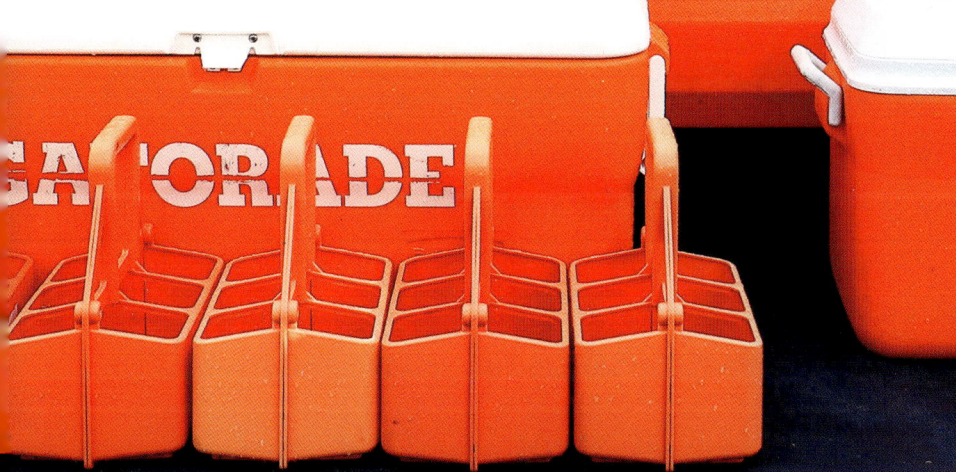

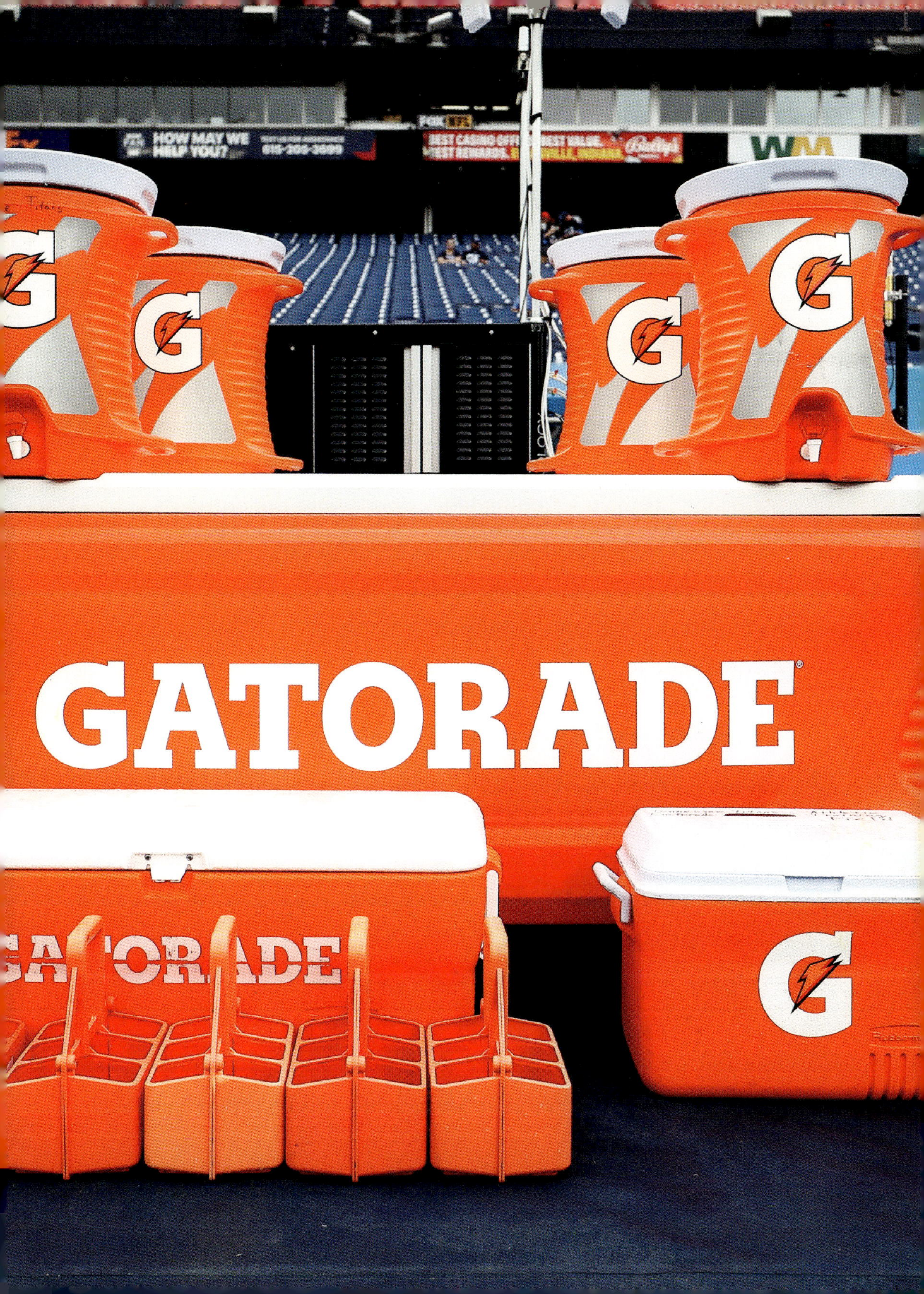
HOW MAY WE
HELP YOU?
WM
GATORADE

Their finish line was the beverage table. Large coolers were stocked with ice-cold bottles of Gatorade. Coach always stressed the importance of staying hydrated. "Drink!" he would yell. "Sip it, gulp it, just get it in."

Charlie and Derrick each grabbed a Gatorade and collapsed to the ground. They held the chilled bottles against their hot, sweaty faces. Charlie consumed his entire bottle in one drink. Orange was his favorite flavor. As a sports drink, the beverage quenched his thirst and refueled his body with the nutrients it needed to stay energized. Charlie whooped, jumping to his feet. "C'mon, Derrick," he exclaimed. "Let's go!" Though Charlie had felt tired only minutes before, he now felt ready to run another lap.

The Popularity of Gatorade

Gatorade began as a beverage for one college's football players in the 1960s. Throughout its existence, Gatorade has long been associated with football. But its appeal is much greater. The drink is popular with athletes of all ages and skill levels in a variety of sports.

Today, the Gatorade brand has a variety of beverage options. These include powdered versions that can be added to water. Consumers can also choose other Gatorade products designed to fuel the body. Options include protein shakes and

Gatorade has many types of products such as energy chews.

Xander Bogaerts of the Boston Red Sox drenches teammate Christian Vazquez with Gatorade after Vazquez hit a home run.

energy chews. People can also buy gear, such as sports bottles, jugs, and towels. Gatorade even has a mobile app and items that sync with it.

Gatorade is more than simply popular. It is the most popular sports drink worldwide. This well-known sports brand accounts for 70 to 80 percent of sports beverage purchases around the globe. Sales are in the billions of dollars each year. In 2021, sales of Gatorade at US convenience stores alone totaled more than $2.5 billion.

The popularity of Gatorade is clear. But while millions of people may know the brand, many may not know its origin. It all started with a college football team, a concerned assistant coach, and a group of scientists.

Gatorade Players of the Year

Every year Gatorade names high school players of the year in each of the 50 states and the District of the Columbia. A committee chooses players in 12 sports based on athletic and academic performances and character. The committee also picks 12 national winners from the state winners, one in each sport. In addition to receiving recognition, winners may choose a local charity to receive $1,000 from Gatorade.

Chapter Two

FOUNDED IN RESEARCH

In the early 1960s, Dwayne Douglas was an assistant football coach for the University of Florida Gators. He noticed dramatic physical changes in his players during practices and games. The athletes were losing a lot of weight. Some players lost up to 18 pounds (8.1 kg) in a day.

Another concern was lack of urination, or peeing. Players also suffered from heatstroke. This happens when the body gets hot and no longer works properly. Heatstroke can be deadly. Florida's high temperatures and humidity made athletes more likely to suffer

Gatorade began its story at the University of Florida.

No Drinking Allowed

Today, coaches make sure players stay hydrated. That was not the case in the 1960s. In fact, coaches did the opposite. They would not let players drink water during practices or games. At best, a player could take a swig of water with a salt tablet. Coaches forbade drinking water because they thought it would make their players slow.

heatstroke than athletes playing football in cooler climates. The additional weight of their football equipment made the situation worse.

Douglas happened to have another role on campus. He was a security officer at the medical school. That is where he met Dr. Robert Cade. Cade was a kidney specialist. Kidneys help transform the body's toxins into urine. The kidneys need to work properly for the body to be healthy. One morning in 1965, Douglas ran into Cade and his colleague, Dr. Dana Shires, another kidney specialist. The two doctors were researchers. Douglas asked Cade why football players were not urinating during games. This simple question would change the scientists' lives.

The Research

Douglas, Cade, and Shires guessed that players might not be urinating because they were sweating so much. If they wanted to help the players, Cade and Shires needed to find out for sure. Two more doctors, H. James Free and Alejandro

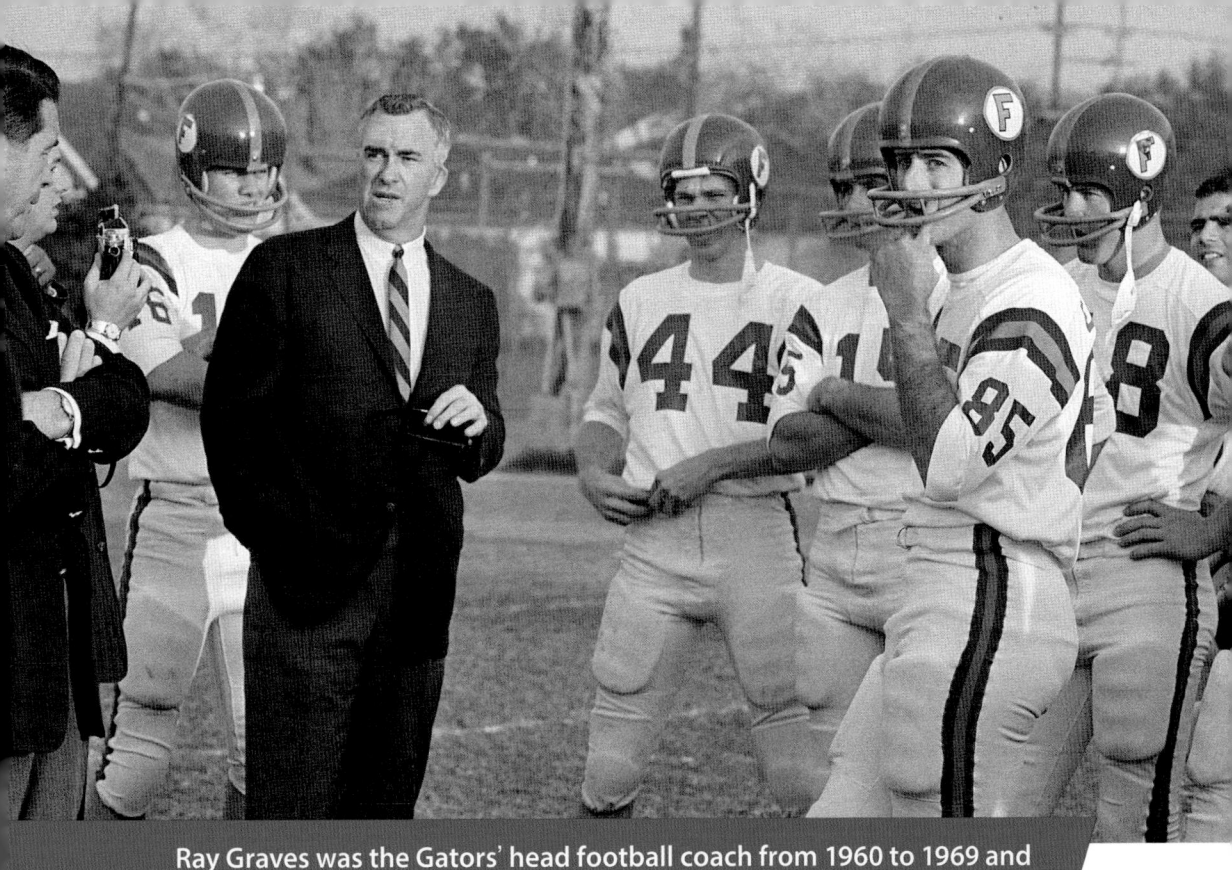

Ray Graves was the Gators' head football coach from 1960 to 1969 and was the university athletic director from 1960 to 1979.

de Quesada, joined the investigation. Together, the four researchers went to Ray Graves, the Gators' head football coach. They asked Graves for permission to study the team. Graves told the group they could study his freshman players.

After the football players practiced, the researchers gathered the Gators' jerseys. Then they squeezed out all the sweat they could from the jerseys. The doctors learned that each player lost 8.1 quarts (7.7 L) of water during the two hours of training.

A Gross Success

Using the data they collected, Cade, Shires, Free, and de Quesada got to work creating a drink for the football team. They wanted the beverage to provide carbohydrates, electrolytes, and salt. Carbohydrates, such as sugar, provide fuel. Electrolytes are minerals, which help move fuel and waste in and out of the body's cells. Salt supports different things, such as muscle movement. The body needs carbohydrates, electrolytes, and salt to function properly. The body also releases these things when it sweats. Cade's challenge was to create a drink that could quickly refuel the body with these important nutrients. The players needed immediate results to keep performing well.

At first, Cade and his team focused on science, not flavor. When three of the doctors tried their first concoction, they spit out the drink. Cade swallowed the sample and vomited immediately.

Athletes drink large amounts of fluids in order to recover water and minerals lost through sweating.

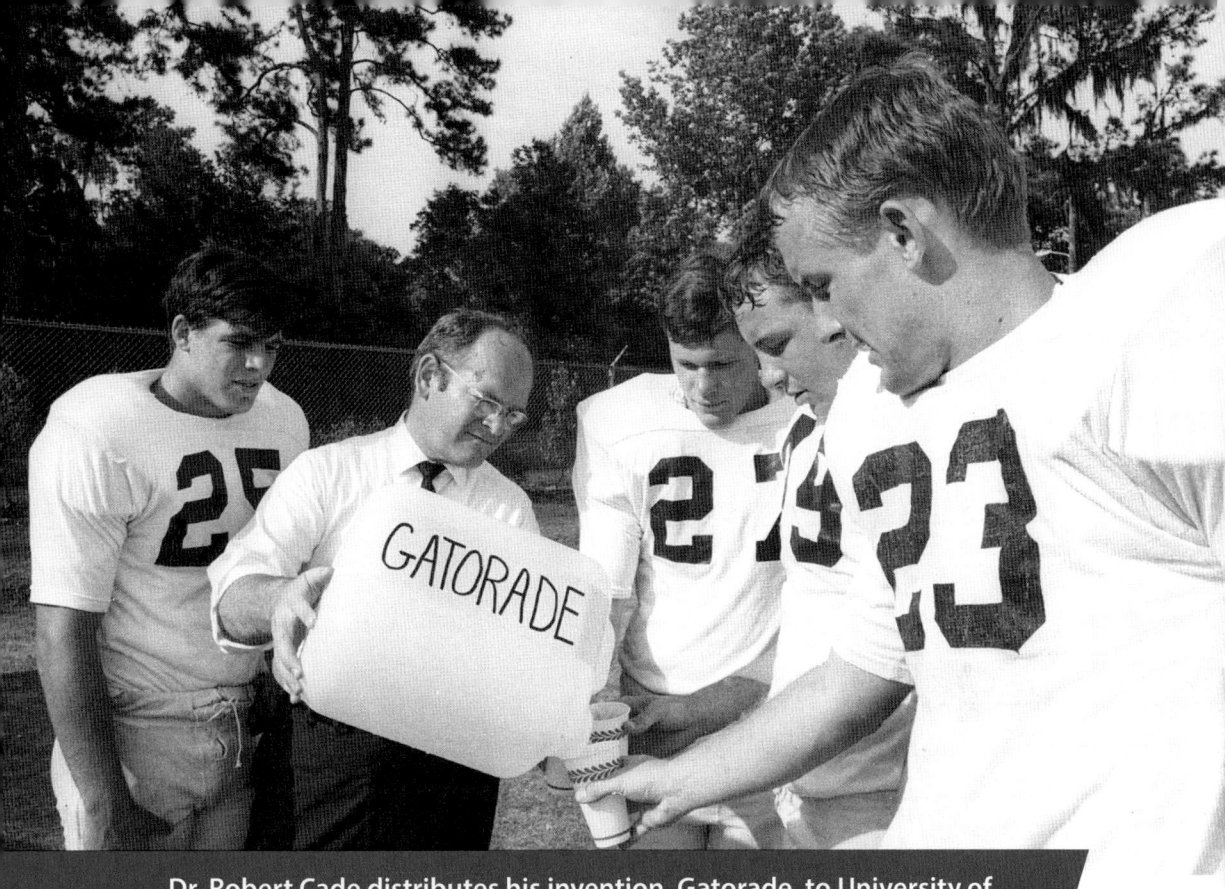
Dr. Robert Cade distributes his invention, Gatorade, to University of Florida football players during a practice.

The scientists tweaked their creation to improve its taste. They added lemon and orange flavors. They also sweetened the beverage. It still did not taste great, but it was tolerable. Then the researchers were ready to test the drink on players.

Cade and his colleagues introduced their concoction to the freshman football team. After drinking the beverage during practices and games, players lost less weight. Fewer players suffered from heat exhaustion. More than that, the team started performing better. The researchers then gave the drink

After Gatorade signed a partnership with the NFL in 1968, players like Green Bay Packers wide receiver James Lofton were spotted with the sports drink in every game.

to the varsity players. The Gators soon noticed an improvement in their performance on the field.

The following year, in 1966, Florida finished the regular season 9–2. That earned the Gators a spot in the prestigious Orange Bowl in Miami, Florida, on January 1, 1967. By then, the team's secret weapon had its name—Gatorade.

Florida defeated a highly favored Georgia Tech team 27–12. Yellow Jackets coach Bobby Dodd offered a simple reason for his team's loss: Gatorade. Florida had it, and Georgia Tech did not.

News about Gatorade quickly made it to other colleges. Several football teams soon had Gatorade on their sidelines every Saturday afternoon. The sports drink was a hit. Next, it would become a commercial product.

> **Gatorade Trust**
>
> Royalties from the sales of Gatorade go to the Gatorade Trust. From there, the money goes to the four researchers who developed it and those they have designated to receive it. The University of Florida gets 20 percent as the result of a legal battle. Since Gatorade hit the market in 1967, royalties have exceeded $1 billion.

Going Commercial

While Gatorade was gaining popularity among college football squads, Shires and de Quesada left Cade's Gatorade team. They got new jobs at Indiana University. Kent Bradley, a doctor and colleague of Cade's, went as well. Eventually, the rights to Cade's sports drink ended up in Indiana too.

Bradley attended a party hosted by Stokely-Van Camp, an Indianapolis company that made canned beans. At the party, Bradley met Alfred J. Stokely and other high-level people from the company. Bradley told them about Gatorade. They wanted to know more. Bradley asked Cade for samples. Cade, who was still in Florida, sent grape, lemon-lime, and orange.

Stokely liked the product and wanted to make it available to all consumers, not just college football teams. In May 1967, Cade, Shires, Free, and de Quesada sold the rights to Gatorade to Stokely-Van Camp. The researchers gave the bean company the product and the name. The men wanted $1 million, but Stokely-Van Camp did not want to pay that much for something that might fail. Instead, Cade and his colleagues would receive a royalty forever.

That summer, product specifics were finalized, including a name. Stokely-Van Camp suggested calling the sports drink Rebound or Quench. But the original name stayed. This was because many people already knew the drink as Gatorade.

Gatorade landed on the commercial market in July 1967. One quart (0.9 L) sold for 29 cents. In 2020 dollars, that amount was equivalent to $2.27. At first, Stokely-Van Camp packaged Gatorade in the same cans used for its beans. That proved to be problematic. The cans rusted inside, which made them leak. The drink ended up making a mess where people stored it.

Realizing their mistake, Stokely-Van Camp made a change immediately. By December, Gatorade was sold in glass jars instead of cans. Stokely-Van Camp advertised Gatorade as the "beverage of champions."

In 1969 Gatorade promoted its drink, saying that 23 football teams and 11 baseball teams drank the beverage.

Since its introduction to the public, Gatorade has changed hands. In 1983 Quaker Oats Co. bought Stokely-Van Camp. Then, in 2001, PepsiCo bought Quaker Oats. As the years have passed, the Gatorade brand has expanded in different ways.

Chapter Three

ENERGY DRINKS AND MORE

Today, Gatorade sells dozens of products. On the company's website, products are split into two categories: fuel and gear. Fuel products focus on hydration, energy, protein, and supplements. Hydration products focus on helping drinkers replenish their bodies after losing water through sweating. In 2022 the original drink was available in 22 flavors. The selection included fruit punch, lime cucumber, lemon-lime, and orange. G2 is another type of drink. It has half the amount of sugar as regular Gatorade while providing the same electrolytes. G2 is available in three flavors.

Gatorade drinks have expanded to include many flavors.

Another drink, Gatorlyte, is designed to help people hydrate themselves faster than the original drink. This option also has less sugar than regular Gatorade. Gatorlyte is available in six flavors.

In 2022 Gatorade introduced a drink called Gatorade Fit. Available in six flavors, it does not have added sugar or artificial colors, flavors, or sweeteners. Gatorade Fit was advertised to be healthier. It has vitamins A and C. The drink contains 4 percent watermelon juice, which accounts for the 1 gram of sugar. Stevia, a plant, sweetens the beverage without adding calories.

In January 2023, Gatorade introduced an energy drink called Gatorade Fast Twitch. It comes in six flavors. It also contains zero sugar and 200 milligrams of caffeine, which is approximately as much caffeine as two cups of coffee. Caffeine is a natural stimulant found in drinks such as coffee and tea. Studies have shown that it can help with exercise performance.

Hydration products also include powders. These powders can be mixed with water. Buyers can also choose pods to add to their Gatorade bottles. To create the sports drink, people can mix water and the contents of a pod to make up to 30 fluid ounces (887 mL) of Gatorade. Using the pods prevents plastic waste from bottles. On its website, Gatorade has instructions to ship the used pods for free so they can be recycled.

Gatorade Fit is advertised to be healthier than regular drinks from Gatorade.

Gatorade's energy products are designed to help athletes prepare for activity. The company also has products that can help people do longer fitness activities. This includes gel pouches, including one with caffeine.

Gatorade also has protein products. These are meant for use after working out. Protein helps build and repair muscle. Gatorade offers a variety of protein products including bars, shakes, and powders.

Dietary supplements give people essential nutrients to support their health. In 2022 Gatorade introduced a dietary supplement line, which included gummy products. One product is called Gatorade Recovery. It is designed to help users' bodies recover from the stress and strain of exercise. Another supplement is called Gatorade Immune Support. This product is filled with vitamins and minerals. It can give the body strength to fight illnesses.

Gear

Gatorade gear includes products other than things people can consume. This includes items such as bottles, coolers, and towels. The brand has different size, style, and color options for individuals and teams.

Gatorade sells all kinds of reusable water bottles. Most of them hold 26 fluid ounces (769 mL) or 30 fluid ounces (887 mL) of liquid. Customers have many designs to choose from. Gatorade has teamed up with the National Basketball Association (NBA) and National Football League (NFL) to give fans customizable bottles with their favorite teams' logos. Customers can also choose to purchase bike bottles. These bottles are designed to fit into the bottle holder on a bicycle.

On its website, Gatorade offers specialized bottles, such as 24-fluid-ounce (710-mL) shaker bottles meant for

Many professional athletes drink from Gatorade reusable bottles, which are also available to the general public.

protein powders. These bottles have a mixing ball that helps mix the drink quickly and completely.

Consumers can purchase containers larger than bottles. Jugs are the next size up. They hold 64 fluid ounces (1,893 mL) of liquid. And sports teams can buy three-gallon (11.4-L) coolers. These bright-orange coolers are a familiar sight on the sidelines at football games. The coolers are also visible on basketball benches, in baseball dugouts, and at other sporting events. The cooler is also a staple for celebrations. After a win, players sometimes dump Gatorade over their coaches' heads.

Technology: Software and Hardware

Gatorade has a mobile app. The Gx App is available for iPhones and offers sports science to all users. Its content focuses on exercise, recovery, and nutrition. For example, the app includes training programs for building strength and completing a marathon. The app encourages recovery by specifying rest days, which are days without workouts.

Specific products are designed to work with the app. The Gx Sweat Patch helps users personalize their experience with the Gx App. The patch sticks to the skin. It provides information about how much the wearer is sweating. It can also show users how much fluid and salt they are losing. Just as Dr. Robert Cade and his team studied football players' sweat in the 1960s, the patch helps wearers understand their bodies better. The patch is intended to be worn once. To get information from the patch, users must scan the patch with their Gx App.

Showered for Success

A frequent sight after a big win in football is the Gatorade shower or Gatorade dunk. It happens when players dump a cooler of Gatorade over their coach's head. The first known occurrence was at a professional football game in 1984. When the New York Giants won the game, defensive lineman Jim Burt dumped a cooler of Gatorade on head coach Bill Parcells.

Gatorade offers a personalized app for people who are interested in sports science.

The Smart Gx Bottle also pairs with the mobile app. Its hardware tracks drinking and helps users record how much liquid they are consuming. The bottle cap has LED lights that help owners easily understand their drinking and better control their hydration. The GX App aims to expand upon Gatorade's goal of supporting athletes in achieving peak performance.

Chapter Four

FOCUSED ON ATHLETES

Gatorade has always been about athletes. In addition to providing products designed to support performance, the brand works with athletes in other ways. Gatorade partners with athletes in a variety of professional sports. Usually, these individuals are at the top of their leagues.

Michael Jordan was the first athlete Gatorade signed to an endorsement deal. The partnership began in 1991 with a 10-year agreement in which Jordan would be paid an average of $1.4 million per year. In exchange, Jordan would promote the brand, including in commercials. In 1992 the "Be Like Mike" TV ad

Gatorade signed Michael Jordan to an endorsement deal in 1991. That same year, he was named the NBA's Most Valuable Player for the second time and also won his first NBA championship.

featuring Jordan drinking Gatorade became iconic. Gatorade saw the power of partnering with Jordan.

Mia Hamm was another important Gatorade partner. Women's sports were growing rapidly during the 1990s. Hamm and the US women's soccer team were at the forefront of that growth. As the team's star forward, she led the team to championships at the World Cup and the Olympic Games. In 1999 Gatorade began a partnership with Hamm to encourage more female athletes. She was Gatorade's first female athlete endorser.

Since Jordan and Hamm, Gatorade has partnered with dozens of professional athletes in the United States. Examples include basketball player Dwayne Wade, tennis player Serena Williams, and golfer Tiger Woods. Gatorade sponsors athletes in other countries too. It partnered with Usain Bolt, a Jamaican sprinter who won eight Olympic gold medals during his career. In Canada, athlete partners include multiple hockey players, including Sidney Crosby and Marie-Philip Poulin. Swimmer Aurélie Rivard and tennis player Bianca Andreescu are part of Gatorade's Canada family too.

Gatorade also sponsors professional sports teams and entire professional sports leagues. This has included the NBA, NFL, and National Hockey League. Gatorade also sponsors leagues in Canada, including the Canadian Football League.

Gatorade had a longstanding relationship with NASCAR that started in 1984.

Gatorade Sports Science Institute

Gatorade also works with athletes in a scientific setting. In 1985 the brand created the Gatorade Sports Science Institute (GSSI). GSSI scientists study athletes at all levels. GSSI's goal is to understand the body to help athletic performance. Researchers study hydration just as Dr. Robert Cade and his colleagues did at the University of Florida.

GSSI scientists also explore other areas. Topics include how environment and exercise affect the body. GSSI's headquarters are in Valhalla, New York. Additional locations are in Bradenton,

Florida, and Frisco, Texas. GSSI also has a location in the United Kingdom.

GSSI works with researchers worldwide, including at universities. Through GSSI, Gatorade has given more than 100 grants to student researchers in several regions of the world. GSSI also strives to share information with doctors, trainers, and others in the sports industry. In all its work, GSSI aims to help athletes be their healthiest and perform their best.

Gatorade Performance Partner

Gatorade focuses on research and sharing information through its Gatorade Performance Partner program. The program gives coaches, trainers, and other sports professionals a place to access current information. Members of the program can also take courses developed by GSSI. Courses are available in areas such as exercise physiology and sports nutrition, among others. For example, one nutrition course discusses how supplements help athletes who play team sports.

Whether it is GSSI or Gatorade Performance Partner, science is the foundation of Gatorade's work. And Gatorade works to make the product of that science available to the public.

Approximately 1,377 athletes participated in the Gatorade Ironman Triathlon on October 19, 1991.

Chapter Five

CONNECTING WITH CONSUMERS

From its start, Gatorade has had a strong reputation. Its positive results for the Florida Gators fueled its initial popularity. The brand's strong association with athletic performance has been constant. And Gatorade's partnerships with athletes have also been important.

Often, people emulate those they admire. So, when a favorite athlete or team drinks Gatorade, many fans will too. Legendary basketball player Michael Jordan was an example. The 1992 "Be Like Mike" TV commercial featuring Jordan was a hit. It encouraged viewers to be like Jordan by drinking Gatorade.

Tampa Bay Buccaneers quarterback Tom Brady takes a drink from a Gatorade bottle before a game.

Paige Bueckers: Gatorade's First College Endorsement

In November 2021, Gatorade partnered with its first college athlete, University of Connecticut women's basketball star Paige Bueckers. Historically, college athletes had been banned from making money on endorsements. That rule changed on July 1, 2021. This was not Gatorade's first time honoring Bueckers. She was the 2019–20 Gatorade National Girls Basketball Player of the Year.

Endorsements can boost Gatorade sales, but the brand encourages consumer engagement in other ways too.

Personalization

People like buying products that reflect themselves and their interests. In fact, buyers usually engage more with brands that offer personalization than with those that do not. Gatorade offers bottles in a variety of colors, patterns, and team logos for people to choose from.

Gatorade's Gx platform takes personalization a step further. It gives users the opportunity to design their own bottles and the pods that go into them. For buyers who want healthier beverages, Gatorade has expanded its drink selection. It offers drinks that have less sugar, include vitamins, and are organic.

Getting People to Play

Gatorade has always focused on helping athletes perform at their best. Besides fueling athletes, the brand seeks to

University of Connecticut guard Paige Bueckers was the first college athlete to sign a partnership with Gatorade.

encourage sports participation. Gatorade launched two initiatives in the early 2020s that focused on increasing participation in sports. The first was the Gatorade Women's Advisory Board.

According to the Women's Sports Foundation, boys have 1.3 million more opportunities to play high school sports than girls do. And by age 14, twice as many girls as boys have stopped playing sports. In 2021, Gatorade launched the Gatorade Women's Advisory Board. All its members are women, and their goal is to encourage girls to play sports. The board launched with 14 members, including several professional and Olympic athletes. Jill Abbott was a founding member. She was Gatorade's head of consumer and athlete engagement. She said of the board, "We have a dedicated group of women from a variety of backgrounds, professions, and stages of life who will help us deepen our connection with female athletes, while also holding us accountable in delivering against our guiding pillars."

In 2022 Gatorade announced another project with a similar focus. Fuel Tomorrow is a multiyear initiative with the goal of increasing kids' participation in sports. The project has a particular focus on youth who are Black, brown, female, LGBTQ+, or from low-income families.

Through Fuel Tomorrow, Gatorade plans to promote playing sports and equal opportunities in sports by concentrating on three things: programs, access, and training. Programs include teaming up with communities and providing youth welcoming places to play. Access is about the availability of sports equipment and transportation to sports facilities. Training focuses on teaching coaches about the importance of promoting equity and inclusion.

Gatorade does not plan to be alone in its venture. The company's goal is to collaborate with several organizations

Gatorade created pink merchandise to bring more awareness to breast cancer.

to have the greatest impact and give as many children as possible opportunities to play sports. Gatorade pledges to give $10 million to these organizations to support their programs. The money is only an initial donation.

Gatorade also plans to work with the DICK's Sporting Goods Foundation. This foundation supports kids who come from high poverty in playing sports. Gatorade will work with other retailers as well, including Walmart. Gatorade's goal in collaborating with these organizations and others is to create community partnerships.

With the Gatorade Women's Advisory Board and Fuel Tomorrow, Gatorade aims to encourage young athletes and help them grow as individuals. Gatorade's community focus has given the company a positive public image. Having a positive brand image can help increase company growth and sales.

Controversies

Countless people consume Gatorade to enjoy its benefits, including kids. However, Gatorade isn't the healthiest choice for nonactive people. Gatorade drinks tend to have high amounts of sugar. They also have food dyes such as Red No. 40 and Yellow No. 5. These dyes may be connected to cancer.

Gatorade's unhealthy ingredients came under the spotlight in 2013. Customers found out that the drinks had brominated vegetable oil (BVO) in them. This ingredient is known as a flame retardant, which is used to prevent or stop fires. BVO is also linked to harmful symptoms. It can cause brain impairment and changes in thyroid hormones.

In 2017 Gatorade was involved in another controversy. The brand faced backlash from the state of California. The company released a smartphone game that promoted drinking Gatorade over drinking water. California sued Gatorade for false advertising. Gatorade paid California a $300,000 settlement. Of that sum, $120,000 went toward studying or promoting nutrition and drinking water for youth.

Is Gatorade Really Healthy?

A 20-fluid-ounce (591-mL) bottle of Gatorade contains 34 grams of sugar.

Gatorade has been criticized as a sports drink for its high amounts of sugar.

Looking Ahead

Despite its flaws, Gatorade has been the sports drink of choice for countless consumers. The company has multiple strengths. It has long-standing products fans love and new items to meet consumers' needs. Gatorade's different projects work to advance sports participation and performance. By continuing to grow and adapt, the company has been able to build on its mission of supporting athletes of all levels.

TIMELINE

1965
Researchers begin studying freshman football players at the University of Florida.

1965
Florida football players begin drinking Gatorade, and their playing improves.

1967
Dr. Robert Cade and his colleagues sign over the rights and name of Gatorade to Stokely-Van Camp, which begins mass-producing the sports drink.

1991
Michael Jordan becomes the first athlete to sign a contract with Gatorade to promote the brand.

1999
Mia Hamm becomes the first female athlete to sign a contract with Gatorade to promote the brand.

2021
In April, Gatorade launches the Gatorade Women's Advisory Board to support girls' participation in sports.

2021
In November, Gatorade signs a partnership with its first college athlete, Paige Bueckers.

2022
Gatorade launches the Fuel Tomorrow initiative to support children playing sports, particularly young people who face barriers to participating.

IMPORTANT PEOPLE

Kent Bradley
Kent Bradley was an associate of Dr. Robert Cade and the other Gatorade researchers. Bradley introduced Gatorade to Alfred J. Stokely, a top person at Stokely-Van Camp, the company that made Gatorade available to the public.

Paige Bueckers
Paige Bueckers, a member of the University of Connecticut's women's basketball team, was the first college athlete to sign a partnership with Gatorade.

Robert Cade
Dr. Robert Cade was the lead researcher in the development of Gatorade.

Alejandro de Quesada
A medical doctor, Alejandro de Quesada was part of the research team that developed Gatorade.

Dwayne Douglas
University of Florida assistant football coach Dwayne Douglas launched the research that led to Gatorade.

James Free
A medical doctor, James Free was part of the research team that developed Gatorade.

Ray Graves

As the head coach of the Florida football team, Ray Graves allowed Dr. Robert Cade and his team of researchers to study the freshman football players.

Mia Hamm

Soccer star Mia Hamm was the first female athlete to endorse Gatorade, signing on in 1999. She is a two-time World Cup champion.

Michael Jordan

Basketball legend Michael Jordan was the first professional athlete to endorse Gatorade. In 1991 he signed a contract to partner with Gatorade for an average of $1.4 million annually.

Dana Shires

Medical doctor Dana Shires was part of the research team that developed Gatorade.

Alfred J. Stokely

Alfred J. Stokely held a top position at Stokely-Van Camp, the canned bean company that made Gatorade available to consumers.

GLOSSARY

carbohydrate
A type of nutrient that provides fuel for the body.

electrolyte
A substance that moves fuel and waste in and out of the body's cells.

emulate
To imitate, or copy, someone.

endorsement
When a celebrity promotes a company in exchange for their products or money.

exercise physiology
The study of how the body responds to exercise.

heatstroke
A condition in which the body becomes overheated and no longer functions properly.

hydrate
To drink enough fluids.

intensity
The degree of a quality, such as how hard someone worked out.

royalty
A payment to someone for something he or she created.

stimulant
Something that makes the body or a body part more active.

supplement
Something taken in addition to food and drink that provides nutrients the body needs.

MORE INFORMATION

BOOKS

Hustad, Douglas. *Innovations in Football*. Minneapolis, MN: Abdo Publishing, 2022.

Jenner, Caryn. *Sports Legends*. New York, NY: DK Publishing, 2019.

Rowell, Rebecca. *Nike: Sportswear and Brand-Building Powerhouse*. Minneapolis, MN: Abdo Publishing, 2024.

ONLINE RESOURCES

To learn more about Gatorade, please visit **abdobooklinks.com** or scan this QR code. These links are routinely monitored and updated to provide the most current information available.

INDEX

Abbott, Jill, 38
Andreescu, Bianca, 30

Bolt, Usain, 30
Bradley, Kent, 17–18
Bueckers, Paige, 36
Burt, Jim, 26

Cade, Dr. Robert, 12, 14–15, 17–18, 26, 31
Crosby, Sidney, 30

de Quesada, Alejandro, 12–14, 17–18
DICK's Sporting Goods Foundation, 39
Douglas, Dwayne, 10, 12

Free, H. James, 12, 14, 18
Fuel Tomorrow, 38–39

G2, 20
Gatorade Fast Twitch, 22
Gatorade Fit, 22

Gatorade Immune Support, 24
Gatorade Performance Partner, 32
Gatorade Player of the Year, 9, 36
Gatorade Recovery, 24
Gatorade Sports Science Institute (GSSI), 31–32
Gatorade Women's Advisory Board, 37–39
Gatorlyte, 22
Graves, Ray, 13
Gx App, 8, 26–27
Gx Sweat Patch, 26

Hamm, Mia, 30

Jordan, Michael, 28–30, 34

Olympic Games, 30

Parcells, Bill, 26
PepsiCo, 19
Poulin, Marie-Philip, 30

Quaker Oats Co., 19

Rivard, Aurélie, 30

Shires, Dana, 12, 14, 17–18
Smart Gx Bottle, 27
Stokely, Alfred J., 17–18
Stokely-Van Camp, 17–19

University of Florida Gators, 10, 13–17, 34

Wade, Dwayne, 30
Williams, Serena, 30
Woods, Tiger, 30
World Cup, 30

ABOUT THE AUTHOR

Rebecca Rowell has put her degree in publishing and writing to work as an editor and as an author, working on dozens of books. Recent topics as an author include the world's wildfires and dealing with family challenges. She lives in Minneapolis, Minnesota.